The

Door

That

Always

Opens

The
Door
That
Always
Opens

POEMS

Julie Funderburk

Louisiana State University Press | Baton Rouge

Published by Louisiana State University Press
Copyright © 2016 by Julie Funderburk
All rights reserved
Manufactured in the United States of America
LSU Press Paperback Original
First printing

Designer: Laura Roubique Gleason
Typefaces: Whitman, text; Livory, display
Printer and binder: LSI

Library of Congress Cataloging-in-Publication Data

Names: Funderburk, Julie, author.
Title: The door that always opens : poems / Julie Funderburk.
Description: Baton Rouge : Louisiana State University Press, [2016]
Identifiers: LCCN 2016008116 | ISBN 978-0-8071-6396-2 (softcover : acid-free
    paper) | ISBN 978-0-8071-6397-9 (pdf) | ISBN 978-0-8071-6398-6 (epub) |
    ISBN 978-0-8071-6399-3 (mobi)
Classification: LCC PS3606.U635 A6 2016 | DDC 811/.6—dc23 LC record
    available at http://lccn.loc.gov/2016008116

for my parents

Contents

Acknowledgments

These poems have appeared previously, sometimes with different form or title. Many thanks to the editors.

32 Poems: "Bonfire" and "Glass Is Not Death"; *Best New Poets* reprinted "Another Consequence of the Storm"; *Birmingham Poetry Review:* "Future Site of Fletcher Academy," "My Family Arrives at the Beach," and "The Spy's Egg"; *Blackbird:* "Lines" and "Planetarium (One Adult Admission)"; *Cave Wall:* the series *New House; The Cincinnati Review:* "An Efficiency in Another Town," "Landscape of the Careful," and "Landscape of the Young"; *Connotation Press: An Online Artifact:* "Dear Regret," "My Father's Family Arrives," and "Slated for Demolition"; *The Greensboro Review:* "Another Consequence of the Storm," "Nothing About Your Life," and "The Search"; *Hampden-Sydney Poetry Review:* "A Girl Reaches" and "Landscape of the Widowed"; *Hayden's Ferry Review:* "Landscape of the Conflicted"; *The Louisville Review:* "Poppies"; *Ploughshares:* "Young Men Playing Dominoes, Pretending to Be Old"; *Signet* reprinted "Pompeii Redux"; *Smartish Pace:* "Notes for Surviving Girlhood"; *South Dakota Review:* "It's My Mother"; *Southern Poetry Review:* "Ping-Pong"; *Third Coast:* "Figure of the Buck"; *Verse Daily* reprinted "Bonfire"; The Waywiser Press reprinted "How I Was Saved," "Landscape of the Conflicted," "Landscape of the Young," and "Pompeii Redux"; *West Branch:* "Ten Years Gone."

Some of these poems appear in the limited-edition chapbook *Thoughts to Fold into Birds* (Unicorn Press, 2014).

I have been deeply fortunate as a student of poetry and wish to thank my teachers and mentors. Thank you Fred Chappell. Thank you Eavan Boland, Jim Clark, Stuart Dischell, Tom Kirby-Smith, Rebecca McClanahan, Michael McFee, James Seay, Alan Shapiro, and Ellen Bryant Voigt.

Heartfelt thanks to my readers. Thank you Renee Soto. Thank you Dan Albergotti, Martin Arnold, David Blair, David Bruzina, Morri Creech, Sarah Creech, Quinn Dalton, Joan Houlihan, Tom C. Hunley, Charles Israel, Kathy Peterson, Craig Renfroe, Susan Sindall, Bruce Snider, and Christina Stoddard.

Thank you John Easterly, Alice Friman, Laura Roubique Gleason, Terry Kennedy, Mike Kobre, Lynn Morton, Erin Rolfs, Alexa Royden, Andrew Saulters, Emily Seelbinder, and Lee Campbell Sioles.

Thank you to all of my family and friends. A special thank you to Amy Funderburk, Carl Funderburk, Jimmy Williams, Audrey Tinsley, Carr Street, and the Clark family.

I am grateful to the Bread Loaf Writers' Conference, the North Carolina Arts Council, Queens University of Charlotte, RopeWalk Writers' Retreat, the Sewanee Writers' Conference, and the UNC Greensboro MFA Writing Program for scholarships and funding.

The author and LSU Press gratefully acknowledge the generous support of the Frances Lightsey Rice Faculty Development Fund at Queens University of Charlotte. Frances Lightsey Rice was an English teacher and a lifelong reader whose love of literature is embodied in these pages.

PART ONE

Slated for Demolition

Enter, says the rental house. It was your toys
cluttering the yard, yours and your sister's yellow room.
You saw the knotty paneled wall when it bloomed
owls and eyeballs. It's all been whitewashed.
Don't stay. There's a mattress on the floor, crushed cans,
the open arms of a greasy jacket. Nobody,
not even you, speaks here now. In the bath, it's the same
pink mosaic tile. Stare a while, the grid rises up.
In the bedroom where your parents slept, the hardwood's
scorched, there's a view through to the sky—
this is what happens. At the bay window, the demo permit hangs
where sheer curtains used to blow their ghosts.

Landscape of the Young

The wind is a choir of all songs. Yours
must be delivered loudly. Hair is messy and mouths
taste like salt. The sand waits for words to be scrawled,
for obscenities to rise like coins
abandoning their secret hoard. The planet is full,
rotating in emptiness. You are young, you are a visitor,
you have taken the flight of weathered stairs.
When you stand still, grains are pulled
from beneath. Instead of sinking, you sense yourself traveling
rapidly ahead. The day has nearly burned off. Shadows
stretch toward each actuality: the wide slats
of the skeletal pier, whales asleep in the water.
Everything suspected is true. Stray gull feather, sunlight
angling across foam, sparkling flecks of shell.
The gunmetal sea, in its deep wish to be blue.

Zuma #8

After a photograph by John Divola, Zuma Beach, Malibu

Smashed windows, a ruined house facing the sea.
Without it, this view wouldn't be framed—
a sunset-silver water. As for the thin walls,
they're mostly white, though somebody sprayed
red paint. Somebody used a crow bar.
This is no cause for pity. With the glass gone,
the stories from the rooms were freed—birds
snapped up plump mouthfuls. Now all of that
sails into the pink. So what if there are vandals.
So what, the hard suitcase on sodden carpeting.
Even in this state, a house offers an inside.
The entrance to board shut. Somewhere to leave.

Our House

A woodpecker
knocks against
the cedar shake:
this is mine,
our house
its territory,
bird that mates
for life, *this is*
mine now
against a dead
branch, and again,
unwinnable
argument.
And now probing
the bark, trusting
the move—*this*
is mine
at the door
that always opens.

Elegy

Cedar, the scent a potent ink, cedar because my mother
    scattered the cones. Then came trees
and her children with a small forest to walk through
    and the bright days that happen—of listening and tripping over roots.
Was she here? What was her voice?
    The cedar scratched my hand as if I burned from the inside
with the life I'd been given, as if I could become dry or old.
    In that hour I can't forget, her breath was the disruption,
her face already changed. I remember footpaths, the quiet
    traveling them. Ghost-blue juniper berries. Ruptured moth sacs.

Landscape of the Careful

The blue line of the world is curving—
you know the high bank is for you,
bank of trees and brush
from which to watch
those who undertook the forbidden, who climbed
down to the water via root and foothold,
down to the boy who holds hostage
a crawfish—will he kill it? A girl cups her hands
to the water, then to her ear. Is the message
pure impulse? Splashes from the others, cheap
shots and harassments, ten feet from the slosh
of rusted cans—the sign clearly posts
NO SWIMMING. Everybody down there is sending up shouts.
On the surface, rings of sunlight swirl in opulence.
The lake floor, if you have not felt the soft
silt of it nor tasted the saltless, vegetable rot
of blackness—the depths call, *Drown, drown if you must.*

New House

1.

THE UNDERTAKING

The man decides to build a house by himself.
Blue snap of a line, steady bubble in the level:
proofs he will shun the American system of debt.
He rises dark-early on Saturdays. He will not stop long
for any holiday, but will drive nails and wait
for paychecks to purchase the expensive pipes.
Neighbors maintain their lawns, assemble hammocks.
When will you finish? they keep asking.
They ask on Sundays, when he sings in the choir.
They seem fascinated that he should study plumbing,
become certified as an electrician. When his son is born,
he plans another story. Then he has poured
the foundation, watched his kids dance on the slab.
He frames the house with the aid of a skeptical nephew.
When his son is six, he compels the boy's labor.
It's best when the family dines where the dining room will be.
For birthdays, his wife ties balloons to ceiling rafters.
His girls sketch dream rooms. He takes the overtime
his shop-boss offers. He fixes the truck. He has fed
12-gauge wire through the studs. His son turns 13,
a true assistant. When the neighbors ask him now,
they grin. But he has stopped being their baritone.
He fabricates his own duct work. No one driving by
can see the accomplishment of his cove lighting.
His children leave for college. At each reckoning,
he feels close. He's achieved the hourless focus,
the perfect room in which he can sit, where he constructs
the precision of his house. Sometimes, he must rip out
then start again, judging workmanship

rather than the days. A man doesn't have to be comfortable.
The sun fades the exterior trim. The soffit grays.
He tapes windows, intending to repaint. Which color?
The sun bakes adhesive to the glass. Vines
make progress, entering his window frames.

2.

NEIGHBORS, UNDER YOUR SCRUTINY
I SING A SONG OF MY FATHER

Know this. His hands were steady, his eyes fixed.
His house surpassed code for the structural, the mechanical,
the electrical. By the time I was old enough to stand behind him
undetected, I watched him work without saying anything—
the man who had tiled that same bathroom three times,
his hair grayed, a man on his knees, brown spots at his temple
and rounded shoulders. I saw his untied black shoe.
Over and again he pried off nearly perfect, ungrouted rows.
Yes, the family suffered, waiting—the question always
When? I had ripped out and reset my feelings over and again.
We would never move in. I saw the droplight
aimed at his wall of right angles. Above us, the infrared lamp
he liked to switch on, showing it off as I looked up.
Know this. The warmth I would feel as I stepped from that bath.

3.

UNDER CONSTRUCTION

One of us could have been hurt, my brother says, remembering
my father managing the feat of the cast-iron tub, of getting it
upstairs. Likely my mother was worried about his back, about the thing
falling. How would most have accomplished this? Not with one
man. We looked on—small assistants. He'd wrapped it around and around
with oiled chains, then hoisted somehow, his voice calling down
to my mother. Now I can remember the weight, hung from a hole
cut for a spiral stair. I had helped to steady it,
great white beast that swung as though it were caught.

4.

SINGULAR SUMMER

We had no certificate of occupancy and kept clothes in bags.
Reason wasn't helping, so I had shut up about it, stuck
with the subfloor, air mattress and hot plate. One cord
hooked us to the grid, the TV kept low, an outlaw
flicker. Light was a snitch that made my father listen
for outsider sounds. His thoughts were the trespassers—
"building inspector" and "fine." My own were brazen
and peering in—at 18, I could think as I pleased
as I brushed teeth in the working sink.
But I followed his protocol. At night, I blocked windows
with heavy plywood sheets—at 18, I faced
the dark yard for him, its tattletale field song
and cars on the street. Mornings, I uncovered the world
where no one knew. Let daylight ward off suspicion.

5.

GIANT-KILLER

Stranger, as long as you've wondered,
I've hated you with your stranger's questions.
My hatred is in my throat, the reason there aren't words.
I don't feel shy. *Just curious,* you say. *Hasn't this house*
sat empty a decade? How awkward you seem
before a child's silence when I will not let you in.
You keep peering about as if a vague wish for explanation
gives you the right. Twelve years, my mother has waited
for the new kitchen. A set of copperware
shines in boxes. The white sun on the day you chose to stop
is your bad luck—it fuels the stalk that attacks the sky.
The green magic of this rage does not wait for nighttime,
its mandate is to grow. You would give me five small beans?
You would have this family starve? I would climb
to your gold. I would come back a third time.

How I Was Saved

"This full-moon eclipse in Virgo is overwhelming,"
proclaims my silly horoscope. "Your feelings intensify for days."
Last night from my doorstep, I stared into an orange moon,
confessing to no one. "Now you must acknowledge what you feel
even if this creates more problems. Now you must surrender
your irrational need for logic." My history with logic is as follows:

Me, underwater, born to that mutable water—no, thicker
than water. Primordial, the status quo of a family of dreamers—
that kind of soup. One day, a light angled through.
I swam for it. When I broke the surface, it gave me oxygen.
I let it fill me, become a boat and oars
for the new rhythm, the sky of stars enabling navigation.
The land I crawled to was solid as reason.

But how deep, how far, myself as origin?
The crash against wreckage. I had gills, I had pearls,
I covered much of the world. I wanted the treasure
sunk in me. Inventor of whale song, I was full of teeth.

Bonfire

First, my boot heels sank.
Then the ground required more—
and I was lying in the damp field

passing around a silver flask,
becoming light with whiskey
but heavy beside the two men I loved.

A night of friends and their singing
to an October bonfire—by morning
it would appear just a blackened space,

this sending forth of countless sparks
and each impulsively alive, unashamed
to glow its panic

against the backdrop of sky.
Here the air carried my impossibilities
made sharp by the cold, thin but rich

with hickory smoke, the unsustainable
surge when logs shifted and cinders
flew, burning for everywhere

at once. The arc of red energy
while it lasted—all I would give
shape to in that field, so awake

to pressure, the sinking denim,
cuff of flannel almost touching
the one I would not touch,

this drawing down, my impress
deepening—it would outlast me there,
this form I left in the field.

Landscape of the Conflicted

If only you were elsewhere. Elsewhere is like
stepping off a curb, thoughtless in that way,
as definite as a car key turned.
Here, the woods eventually open
to a pond and a waterbird
and then the necessary takeoff: wings stretched wide
to lift the dragging feet, the water
dividing, folding over—two
glittering selves, nymphs arching their backs.
Possibilities are suspended
within this fountain of brightness.
Choose, and you can be seated at a restaurant,
tables of tea lights
reflected in stemware, and in the long wall mirror
all the white napkins.
Choose, and there you'll sit
with an etiquette of silver and a sense of belonging
elsewhere. Elsewhere is like leaning back on a blanket
on the beach where you're supposed to be
watching the tiny lives
wash in, carried there and crawling under.

My Family Arrives at the Beach

On cold sand, we want ghosts, the coast
full of desires so strong they can't leave.
New yet familiar, the salt air and waves—
memory is rejoining the physical. We know this place.
Crabs scuttle across our beams.
The Gray Ghost who is faceless
warns of storms and wants us gone. Love is often death's
undisputed cause, as with The Bride
who hunts the ring her elder brother flung to the sea.
She's a figment veil, the caps beneath the moon.
Our father who is telling these stories
lets her voice wail: "I want my *ring*. *Give* me my *ring*."
He is tall to us and happy at the start
of a long-deserved trip. He knows how to shape
vacated destiny. He leads us toward a lit pier
miles distant, insisting that the ring will wash up there.
We can't get that far. But its thwarted promise,
a circle unlived, is a diamond we believe in.
If it takes years, we'll wait the years it takes him
to show us, our father who whispers
in ears. On the dark beach, we laugh as he taps
us on the back, his moaning making us scream.

Dear Regret,

We lived there with a rough stair. We did not require finish work. My signature scent was your hot attic, where I hung my dresses on a wire.

In your rafters, *wood* became *would*, my family mistaking you for hope, the future setting out from rolled plans, the unfinished house of you.

I owe you. You kept my mind humming in sleepless hours. In the morning I could control neither the content nor the clocks.

Years and years may elapse. But with you, conversations are blooming sunflowers as tall as people, nodding their heads—agreement all around, a little golden finch.

A chandelier, centered without a table—I grew, I moved, taking it with me, packing it myself. Wrapped in a box, its brass was shining, its spider legs an idol.

An old car in the woods—I saw springs pushing through the bench-seat like roots. The steering wheel, woven with needles. Rust accentuating the lingering paint, its blue sky, its pure pool.

I'm sorry. I'm saying goodbye from the swing on my new porch. I'm holding to the chains.

You are wish, but not the coins in the water, not coins in the air. You are in the pocket, where it starts. You are wish, but not the thin candles lit. You are in the mouth, with the held breath—where what we don't have is forming.

Figure of the Buck

Think of a buck
within city limits, surrounded by houses,
blocked in by commuter roads.

An emotion can be relegated to woods without water.
A person can keep questioning whether it's real.

Having found what resembled a track,
I did not make myself a fool for the possibility.
Mornings I did not hunt for scrapes
against the oaks' silver lichen, did not imagine divots

or keep myself motionless
where the animal might have stood.

At the tree line, one night I thought I saw glowing eyes

but was not obliged to react, given the uncertainty.
I could have set out salt
or an offering of hard apples

and now I wonder: close, how much closer
toward my house, from cedar and pine
into the clearing, the moon
barely letting on, did the buck come, legs
back-kicked high, the white stars
expansive over need
expressed there in full:

a frenzied tearing into dirt, antlers
shaking out circles, while I slept,
the heart beating nearby.

PART TWO

Landscape of the Hesitant

You don't take your eyes off the gulls.
In the strip-mall parking lot, they glide from streetlights,
dive for Cheetos and apple cores. Theirs has never been
a kingdom of wild dune grass—
a place you know. You've been to the sea. In waves
their flight forms what they miss, these bodies that summon
wherever they are, however much they need
the great roaring, its bounty of fish. Brute calls
mobbing the world—they do not wait.

Young Men Playing Dominoes, Pretending to Be Old

On purpose they play an old man's game,
grin through cigars, wear stupid hats.

These, who've owned the summer
shirtlessly, inseparably, consuming whatever's

cheap, now swill an aged Scotch
as if long practiced.

They aren't thinking of their current lives
as only a few years' stop-over

till the next thing they'll do, the next—
these simple, work-free afternoons

just a single, roving note—
or they would not pull those dark socks

halfway up their calves,
not even in jest.

How is it they draw from their bone pile
feigning mock-decades, the ever-

evolving sleights, as if they won't lose
in the decades to come

even so much as each other?
Right in front of them, black spots match,

ivory tiles link, connections prove
subject to forces that will and do propel.

Lines stretch ahead
domino by domino, limiting

what had once felt certain,
like days that no longer seem given

but taken. These slouching shapes
slapping their knees, these with strange, shaky voices

should be unable to figure themselves
here, how?

Attempts at Flight

He's as awkward as his outdated moustache,
running then jumping on, pedaling

furiously in a suit, as if in retreat from the word "folly,"

and sometimes pumping with the hand to make those big wings flap—

Grainy footage of failed attempts, for viewing pleasure
set to piano music, because films were silent then—

At least he can't be interrogated
here in posterity, on the bridge with an unwieldy glider

then down in the water, climbing out with the drips—
but he isn't spared "The Entertainer," which seems to speed along

the mishaps, which honor none of his hours
with ink and paper, the welding sparks, the voicing of possibility.

Only the definitive moment—the lighting
of a backpack of explosives, the men in squat

position—he has endeavored. He is ready.
In seconds he is stuck, crashed, proven wrong,

then it's on to the next in this little mishmash.
I will keep rooting for him,

for the contraption to send the creator
where his mind has long been, where this Moses cannot venture—

off the cherry tree's sturdy branch, off the dull

hill, the ubiquitous roof, into never tasted winds.

Planetarium (One Adult Admission)

An hour lets me duck out of my situation.

The planetarium: a den from the afternoon sunlight,
this low sun of December,
my reaching shadows.

When the night sky was my wishing place
and my back contoured the ground,
I pulled at the grass
mindlessly, wanting—

I still keep a sense of restriction:
I can't do what I want.

The dome is a model. Its hunter
desired a moon goddess. Why not let love
be that simple? In his mythic death

he burns his belt of stars.

The lenses shift, configuring the sky,
any time and place the technician decides,
the seasons advancing, their fast spin.
In this turning, here's the view from Sydney:
Scorpius no longer trolling the horizon.

Night sky, when desire stays
only desire, there's a privacy
I wish to renounce.
I wish to accept the risk: once something happens,
the stars there become fixed:

the Christ star
as seen by wise men.

After, there's no real going back.
Physics can't be avoided.

As a star never is
as it appears
when it appears,
by the time its light arrives,
so the brightest never satisfies.

Trying to Light Charcoal in a Coastal Night Wind

In a miasma of fumes, my brother said, *More starter fluid.*
Unafraid of an idea, he said, *Let's use cardboard for a shield.*
Try newspaper. Try moving the grill beneath the deck.
That's when I saw: we had ignited our father.
Of course he'd want to be here, taking care
of our mother, having just taken over my brother,
forehead and nose, inflection and tone.
Man with the matchbook, he intended those sparks
to catch. How much I had missed him. His hands were black
with that stubbornness to achieve when it was time to give it up.
Certain coals had whitened, though the whole kettle
smelled cold. People were hungry—
I doused the grill. We took the raw food in.

My Father's Family Arrives

At 22, I should understand why they've come
rattling the cups in our kitchen.
In his room, made strange
by the oxygen tank, where his open eyes
are not quite his, in a whisper
they ask if he can hear. He can't talk, I say,
but he can hear. My father, always
more sociable than he realized.
Now I am his voice. I do not see
the tumor as the threat—but instead,
the snickering questions they might ask.
That is the critical danger he trained me for,
as apparent as a spot on a brain scan. I am ready.
But our visitors are kind, share a memory
of his mother's cake, nodding at him
when they speak. He loves
you too, I say with my calm certainty.

Another Consequence of the Storm

Our neighbors lost two Bradford pears,
trees that often survive just seven years

(*life of a marriage these days* was the joke),
sending up green, the tear shape

practically begging the wind.
And for three days you and I have stayed

near each other—in the flickering meals, our talk
feeling again like secret exchange.

Tonight we wait in the city-dark;
a fallen magnolia splits the backyard.

We relax in its branches
as if we've climbed, but we've earned nothing,

running our hands along its bark
as if discovery will come: precious little,

a dim white flower, a bowl that holds
the strangeness of all I do not know of you.

Apartment

An arm reaching
out and up

to knock, a body
foreshortened

by the peep-hole.
It was my friend,

and all the black
space between us

visible, encircling
the view. She was

unexpected.
We were in high school.

I tried not to breathe—
on my side, the worn

and the undusted
lamps, couch,

the newspapers
left on the floor

with a path through,
the kitchen stacked—

until she withdrew.

An Efficiency in Another Town

Built-ins lined the walls,
a natural wood
I might have stocked with books,

but my books remained at home,

here, with my whole closet of clothes.
There, stray hangers
would fall from the bar

when I reached. In that room,

light filled the two windows.
I could rest in the one chair
in a cross breeze

and hardly feel strange just sitting.

I could spy as the neighbors
drove away or lit their grills.
For trash day, they pared down,

and I looked forward to the nights

when the man across the alley
kept to himself and his four candles. I wanted
no love but this.

No ringing phone. No hello kiss.

The room meant a breathable relief:
unscented soap or cotton,
a tray of ice.

The tiny kitchen meant the sound,

then steam, of boiling,
then the dry noodles splayed
in the burned, loose-handled pot:

these were the steps

toward sustenance. Before I could
achieve them, I imagined them
over and over

under the heavy

blanket I kept there, my body
a bareness in the room
where I lived off and on.

Another House

Had I known firefighters would burn it down for practice,
I'd have returned to watch and to breathe particles from timbers
my great-great grandfather milled. A spectacle, the brigade rushing in as if to save
the '20s asbestos siding, '50s drop ceiling panels, the carpet fibers of the '70s
aflame without my laboring through asthma, feeling I should be there. For one,
I possess its marble-top Eastlake dresser. For another, my aunt and mother
were born in its front parlor, walls shaped by fire at the last. As our heavy
smoke dispersed, as the beams snapped as it sank, the passing traffic slowed.

Landscape of the Siblings

Above is father sky, beneath is mother earth,
the rain that cycles between. You get the jokes. Around you,
homestead and apple tree, all is overgrown. Together you breathe.
You bury each other's fury in the dry garden of shooter weeds.
Siblings, that time you ran so fast? You'd lifted a warped board
in the shed, saw the snake's gleaming, red-and-black bands.
Poisonous or not—the answer depends. You know where the empty
flower pots get stacked, where the Galaxy rusts. This is where
you held to the tent poles, the family in the wind. This is the meadow,
with its peculiar seedpods, where only you have lain.

Unfinished

1.

TEN YEARS GONE

A stray dog approaches low to the ground,
his coat the color I want:

my father's tan cardigan, the memory of him
leaning from a straight-back chair

beginning to polish his shoes.
My hesitation to call to the dog—eyes that suspect

we do not belong to each other—
becomes enough, long enough for him

to disappear into the neighbor's bamboo,
stealing away, and I've let him,

and watch the stalks
tremble green where he's gone.

2.

13 ACRES OF PROPERTY TAX

Checking on the house for our mother,
accustomed to walls without baseboards, slab flooring,
light fixtures installed as if they could simply switch on,
we seemed to wait for the last daylight hour
and walked around shadows. For a long time, cans of Diet Coke,
a bar of soap, his pencil markings of measurements.
Once in a while, a broken window, a door jamb
busted through. Why hadn't we boxed up his circular saw?
No house can be vacant without the occasional invading animal.
We moved between those rooms as if exploring
the contract between our parents: she never insisted
he hire a crew; he never asked her to sell a parcel
or use land as collateral. A storm, a small leak,
and sheetrock mildews. A ceiling caves. Trees press
against fogged windows to watch: the people are leaving,
their pathway lost to katydids and singing frogs.

3.

AFTER WE SIGN THE PAPERS TO SELL

I emerge through an opening meant for a chimney
before the house plans changed. My feet
balanced on rafters, I picture my father
taking pains to line the dark shingles,
his hammer deft, galvanized nails, course
after course. I climb up, crawl out to touch
the hot, abrasive roof. After a childhood
craning my neck, I see very well the old pin oak.
The acres are simply acres, the summer woods
not so deep. And across the road, down a hill
on a street, misfortune: a neighbor's fire
sends up its black smoke. Wind carries the sirens.

4.

FUTURE SITE OF FLETCHER ACADEMY

After a house is razed, a foundation loaded off,
after the surface is leveled,
woods chipped to a scattered mulch—

rather than pace on top of trees I once climbed,
if I sink,
if I penetrate the new footing,

farther under, still safe,
hides the deepest of fossils, of ancient
burials, someone else's code of ritual—

but the land my mother's family farmed,
the woods I have known,
when those roots

are torn. The severed links
between world and underworld.
When there are no nerves signaling.

After a bulldozer,
after the family's effects,
a mere inch down: ring, horseshoe,

buffalo nickel—once these are scraped
and driven off, what
of recent life? Expunged not by time

but by layer, its tilling of the garden.
Vanished in vanished rows, its dropped watch.
The sole proof of a bare wrist.

5.

TESTIMONY

What it was like, the street as always, nighttime in all its hues,
but the woods cleared. Now a row of startled backyards.
I kept myself standing. It was dark where I was
at the center. I was howling words
not even true, everything was not gone.
What it was like, acres of proof, absent trees and structures
making for difficult markers
as I calculated where the house had been
a fact all my life.
There were a few bricks intact, not carted off,
which I took, which did not feel like stealing.
I thought I saw someone
on the outskirts, tall and listening,
did I? The changes drew us out. It was a reckoning
for apple tree for garden for front door.
The encircling streetlamps blazing
like a constellation, the constancy between them
established that where we were
is where we had been before.

PART THREE

The Spy's Egg

A sixteenth-century spy
      communicated by egg
stolen from the hen
      then boiled and cooled
in a kitchen of scullery maids
      where a message was slyly
penned—the ingenious
      ink seeping through shell
onto the cooked white
      interior of this marvel
kept from routine eggs
      then tucked into a private
apron. Next morning
      through iron gates to travel
in a pocket—never
      handled needlessly
but always as felt weight
      conveyed down the alley
beneath the open shutters
      through bright, jarring streets
to the point of delivery
      where it was cracked.
To be read, it must be peeled.
      Hope for understanding,
warned the spy's egg,
      when the subterfuge ends.

Exposé

Protecting a body after death can mean washing it, or burning it, can mean not leaving it,

and now means searching embalmers for cameras, obtaining signatures on agreements, ensuring personnel make no attempt to draw the body of Anna Nicole Smith.

What kind of world do we live in? some ask. *At last,* they say. Here is the police tape not to cross for money: the medical and/or sacred. We must not conflate Henry Gray's surface anatomy engravings with a recognizable body.

Even hers? some ask. *Alas,* they say. This woman can be pinned up but not pinned down. In the legal document she is Vickie Lynn Marshall. On the prescription pad for methadone, she is Michelle Chase.

An Old World rendering of a geographic edge: unfurled and waiting is a mythic creature perceived by no one yet.

Embalmers, please, do not sketch this body. Let anonymity keep its maps. Even a death

mask is a mask. I was witness once. There is no question. The self is gone from question.

Notes for Surviving Girlhood

When you falter, when you talk

back—an infraction—

accept the punishment, weed the garden, keep your mouth

shut. Do not throw your fistful

of dandelion at the house.

No one can uproot your nerve

if you withhold those light seeds.

Volunteer. Be a helper. Slice the carrots for dinner—

each circle a small, hard sun, the days ahead.

Fear will be taught: walking alone ever,

fatness, ugliness, the unfastened

latch, touching yourself.

You must keep defiance

a window, open to the night, a place for crawling out.

For now, review the materials they want you to see:

in slick picture books: purebreds, the combed

mane of a white horse, the stabled

Arabian. No one suspects

you of becoming the rider

who presses taut

against that muscle.

Pleasures have been ruled

forbidden, therefore the trail you find—let it

be hidden. Scraping through briars,

legs feel alive. Blackberries wait

sour and ripe. Among wet leaves, the shaded

earth, you will trot high above

the white underbellies of the mushrooms.

With only sticks to snap approval.

Nothing About Your Life

Let's say you're visiting an old friend at a beach.
It's October, and excluding the standard update,

your friend knows nothing about your life
(this is your vacation). Let's say beachcombers,

wearing light jackets and shorts, are watching you:
wading at first, you let the cold

water splash, holding your skirt higher.
At the next wave, you duck under.

Visible now: the bra beneath your shirt.
You are the picture of willingness to brave

change, the temperature that shocks. Another wave
hits. You are inside, where drowning is possible,

the gray sea crashing around you,
fish you can't see brushing your legs

(nobody's the wiser). From the shore,
you hear your friend's daughters

shouting your name like the name of a new crush.
Everybody likes the person who just heads in.

They're cheering as you exit the surf
still too far away for them to see

you shivering in the wind-chilled weight of your clothes.

It's My Mother

who stands in the garden, her children
clustered around her, the unfamiliar
children of the school year, watching
the butterflies' release. I hear her teacher-voice,
this woman of the outside world, the insect
feet of that world, its milkweed
and cloud-covered sun

where a person is free
from all that attaches to a family over time.
The butterflies cover her, alight
on her face. One pulses in her hair
as if weighing the minutes.
A Painted Lady on her outstretched finger,
she could be any mother

smiling at these who cannot bear
to leave, these who prove
their affection: she
who brought sugar water. She
who has been mine, who lets
others take from her
while I fail to make myself known.

Landscape of the Widowed

Seasons the field is just a cropped stubble, the wind
can be trusted, the wind is here. And when it blows
a bendable wheat, there's no need for belief—the golden
rolling as beautiful as the mind, remembering.
Sometimes, a gift from the windy field,
a form glimpsed on a plain day, a form in overalls,
in a red plaid shirt. This is not the first
time you are fooled, lengthening confusion, a blur
as black crows alight, fidelity not frightening, arms
pointed east and west, creating its own center, allowing.

Glass Is Not Death

unless you intentionally eat it
then file insurance claims

blaming the restaurant
that did not serve glass in your chowder,

unless the internal injuries go untreated,
which they don't

because you receive expert
medical care before fleeing Rhode Island

for Virginia, where you and your lover
begin assumed lives, the names

sharp and clear in the motel
just off the trail, the loudness of I-95

like the unsatisfied anger of the duped
who can't begin to guess the true

measure of two who understand: glass is death
when, as if into a looking glass

you stare into his glassy eyes, this man
who could end you with a phone call—

Claire, you speak the new word for yourself
as you drink together from cans.

Lines

tell me
the smooth box
rendered by the gloved
hands of a mime

tell me
the spinning particles
between your foot and my foot
each propped on the railing
tell me that nervous inch

tell me yellow
that lines up nevertheless
perennials burning
for their lost house

tell me oxygen
from a cooler layer
unsuitable for
the breath you must take
to tell me

I've scripted
your intimate talk in my head
speak it back

tell me
white butcher paper
the tongue wrapped
separate from the heart

Ping-Pong

From my spot, seated on the floor, the table
appears larger, the sound louder: father to son,

son to father, the secret knock of friendship.
But I will play, and my turn too

will mean my father's mojo shot.
So why should I complain? Under his spell,

from my paddle the ball always ricochets
as if not fully intended for me,

Sweet Pea, nickname meant
as an endearment—see how I am made

small and hard by it? Not a Princess,
instead the Pea, buried beneath the mattresses.

My ambition presses. Then it's my brother
who waits. The ball fits my palm,

unbreakable there, my sly emissary
to ease over the net, light as a mosquito,

fingernail thin in the corner of the room
where it goes when I return the serve

too hard again, its bounce
tapping, its pace quickening.

Poppies

Our friend wants to explain the color he saw
along the highway. It's Mother's Day,
his mother having passed not a month ago,
and he gathers with us, with our mother.
He rocks the glider across from where we grill
peppers on skewers: orange, yellow, green.
We stare into coals as he tries again: "Not just red.
more orange than that," but also somehow "brick."
Our conversation could be small-talk
except for his urgency to tell this red—a *pang,*
or an *aliveness,* though he doesn't have the words,
just the stretch of narrow field, red
that lives in an open place, the length of it
rushed by. We nod, though we don't understand.
Color fills his throat.

The Search

One more rainless day, the lake conceals less and less,
exposure changing everything—footprints left deep
where they would have been underneath—the lake as unreflective
as its belly of mud. Here are roots, the tree long dead. Here are pale bottles
and fish heads. The careless tossed their cans. The rusted anchor
held too well, so the rope snapped, lost a disappointed boat. In this lake,
there is no magical sword, no invisible house. Will the wounds be healed?
Clustered on a stick, soft eggs are the glazed eyes that foresee
this world is a challenge. Its truth has a scent—this is it, the air that tastes
of silt, the water's weight swallowed, the sun in a haze. A couple walks
the widened beach, the lady saying, *Here I am. What will you do?*

A Girl Reaches

for a cloth hung above the well
and falls from the world
of dust and faces. Her palms
find a ledge—a shaky handstand.
Outside, her brother shouts—
he's running, calling to the field
where she should be,
where heat distorts the rows
where bending leads, the glaring cotton.
Inside this mineral coolness
her hair's on end, blood flowing
to her ears. Water a radiant
moon above. Each breath
the taste of an underworld seed.
Not enough to keep her.
She is delivered into the story
she hears then tells in the years,
what the others saw—
her legs kicked air, bare feet
splayed. They grabbed
her ankles, is what they said,
they pulled her back.

Landscape of the Uncertain

The plantings at your front door are untended, a real thicket.
Now spring's choking vine. Within that ribcage,
winter's camellia bloom, dried and browned.
How it embodies terror and pleasure.
You have made your choice. The months ahead
are indeterminate. A month ago, life was possibly perfect.
Let there come numerous handwritten notes imploring
Whatever has possessed you, someone else's thoughts
to fold into birds, a night filled with fluttering.
Along your street of budded trees, the roofs
steeply pitched, the thrill comes from pacing, you are silver
and these are windows and windows of crouching neighbors.
Let them see you—bare feet on a center line
reaching for the luxury of not knowing, isn't it?
The moon keeps low. The stripe feels smooth.

Pompeii Redux

Goddess of bungalows,
of the horseshoe pitch, of couches dragged to front yards,
coming back here has triggered disaster. My hands shake.
I remember that time as windy, a swing chained in place
for a storm, magnolia leaves flipping like playing cards.
And the stories—as if Big Jane's ghost
still rocked on the porch boards, we dared search
for her groove marks. Goddess of chimes, of dog tags,
of nights that tapped because someone hooked empties
to the tree branches: which one of us fell into the pit
before the pig roast? Any weakness of mine kept as silent
as the bricks beneath the pavement, everybody
barefoot, everybody dancing in a gushing rain.
In your everlasting hindsight, even a plate
is an omen. Here is a seed of what we used to eat.
Goddess of ash, here is my crouching shape.

CPSIA information can be obtained
at www.ICGtesting.com
Printed in the USA
LVOW11s1521281016

510723LV00004B/513/P